Always Find the Lesson

PERSEVERANCE JOURNEY

Rochelle W. Kelly

WESTBOW
PRESS®
A DIVISION OF THOMAS NELSON
& ZONDERVAN

WestBow Press books may be ordered through booksellers or by contacting:

WestBow Press
A Division of Thomas Nelson & Zondervan
1663 Liberty Drive
Bloomington, IN 47403
www.westbowpress.com
844-714-3454

ISBN: 978-1-6642-9116-4 (sc)
ISBN: 978-1-6642-9115-7 (e)

Library of Congress Control Number: 2023901733

Print information available on the last page.

WestBow Press rev. date: 2/28/2023

Acknowledgement of Family Friends Community

Always Find The Lesson : Proserity Faith
Rochelle Kelly Author
Westbow Publication Division Thomas Nelson &Zondervan

The persons for my purpose Dedication pages

For whom provision promises power passion providence coming in living

Because you'll taught excellence while inconsister motion Ruby N. Allen

This Grace rise Faith Love rise rise coming in living because the lesson

Excellences consistent motions B. Charles Nelson

Always Find the Lesson

PERSEVERANCE JOURNEY

The johnny Lisa Journey after her travailing continuing with that excellent circumstances.

Those issues are with testing still God(through Father son Jesus Christ NazarethHoly Spirit) is in control while he living existence For instance I am, in various learning modalities listening,celebrations, visional Mathematical. Johnny Lisa was the loves each other because of what was started in them by God through Jesus christ Nazareth

Nevertheless Johnny Lisa has gone their separate ways she made hope that they see each other again.

Nevertheless, John Lisa stay in their academic acknowledgement that made their lives worth living. This is the admiration that they both had for circumstance greater than themselves, yet this white from oldest to youngest couples never gave up longing with each other and without each other. The epic was example,

When she had to to come up in conference with him. (The victory while in the valley during the valley t this is temporary the scripture used Acts 6-7 Ryrie KJV The word of God increased and the number of disciples multiplied in Jersalem greatly and a great company of the priests were obedient to the faith.

Love that Johnny Lisa expand during the test trying to see if they could live with while growing in their lives.

They knew that could perervance through the difficult. Sow they could be together in this life.

Dwight was whom the taught lessons that mostly triumphed in continuing Life.

Nevertheless our journey was adventurous through this was lasting a long time. This is Greater Victory with no clear consequences for failure. Although she/he learned endurance while Being human united when vulernability occurred. He/she went to various places while loving each other such as (museums all over the world) Grace is all that God (Father while he was in on Holy Spirit has done and will do because of what Jesus christ did.

The adventure with Johnny/Jill while they were waiting to be together again.

She/He are in their building circumstances during what the Lord God parpairing both to do.

The relationship (marriage was definitely near) Scripturise: Mark10:9 KJV with TESJ(Tony E). what god joins together let no one put a sunder.

> Note; formula

E - ever
Q - movethis quickly
U - Keep my head up seeking GOD
A - Around God's ominous
T - Total Praise keep praising
I - Never Alone
O - Oh it hurts for a little
N - need my faith to raise

God is with us(the cultures of people of African decent includes Phillipans Asian Hispanic).

This is building living while in purpose . Scripture: 2 Corinthians 3:17 now the lord is the spirit and where the spirit of the lord is there is Freedom.

Now if the ministry that brought condemnation had glory, the ministry that brings righteousness overflows with even more glory . infact, what has been glorious has not been glorious by comparison because of the glory that surpasses it. 2 Corithians 3: 9-10 KJV TES(Tony Evans StudyBible)

The small battles in life prepares us for the big ones or even war . Give an example Of a time reasonly that I was a family member trying to controlling that I believe that

Romance that has that expanded while of neither m knew it would be creating a a sustainability in both of us. Johnny got a another position . Lisa had to stay in her position.

The Continuous learning through came when Lisa met William during a summer1 session at the university most of their mutual friends were gone. We were both taking courses so we could graduate early. We meeting in various places having conversations about our ideas also dreams for whe met hat we doing in our lives then also in the future. William had thousands of women that wanted to be with him because the way he looked not because his ideas with his contribution with his organization because of the conversations only William became the interested in Lisa unaware to her, the semester started ans Lisa was seeking a friend to assit her with statistic . she met a friend name Greggory he was very knowledgeable in this area. She met him mostly in the Library . on one occasion she went to met him at Greg apartment when she got there his room mate was William. William was so upset that I was there to see greg rather than him.

Little children, you are from God and have overcome them, for he who is in you is greater than he who is in the world Scripture : 1 John 4:4 ESV is/was and going to be

Lisa had never met to hurt William unaware of his was feeling. The friend ship was of value only for a season note; lifetime with him. Got to get an understanding of that more. William got that understanding eventually.

That season was short and the next semester started this was Lisa next to last semester before becoming an graduate. Unforeseen to her she met a scholar in Dwight This was one chosen to increase Lisa's daily knowledge of what is going and the future would be the relationship was about creating systems of extensions.

> A faithful Friend is shelter
> A whoever found one
> Has a rare Teasure !
> Eccleiasticus 6;14

Establishing a learning environment that was their goals with together of fundamental systems, Blooming systems, Software systems, people systems . The interesting about Lisa being with Dwight

The eccentric ideas we're constantly flowing with relationship.

The relationship (marriage was definitely near) Scriptures: Mark10:9 KJV with TESB(Tony Evans). what god joins together let no one put a sunder. Note; formula

- ➤ O-not all about me
- ➤ M-unmerited favor of God
- ➤ I-inJesus christ
- ➤ N-near me is Jesus Christ
- ➤ O-it hurts a little while
- ➤ U-undeniable god is near
- ➤ S-significant God loves me,you
- ➤ E-ever in Jesus Ch bist

Q - move this quickly
U - Keep my head up seeking GOD
B - Around God's ominous
T - Total Praise keep praising
I - I NevIer Alone
O - Oh it hurts for a little
N - need my faith to raise

God is with us(the cultures of people of African decent includes Phillipans Asian Hispanic).

This is building living while in purpose . Scripture: 2 Corinthians 3:17 now the lord is the spirit and where the spirit of the lord is there is Freedom.

Now if the ministry that brought condemnation had glory, the ministry that brings righteousness overflows with even more glory . infact, what has been glorious has not been glorious by comparison because of the glory that surpasses it. 2 Corithians 3: 9-10 KJV TESB(Tony Evans StudyBible)

The small battles in life prepares us for the big ones or even war . Give an example Of a time reason that I was a family member trying to controlling insurmountable circumstances I believe now that God's supernatural sprit could complete this resolution.

Nevertheless this was during a moment when Jill/Johnny was getting preparation to leave each other for the first time. They were both feeling some separation anxiety yet they were encourage to continue their initial training knowing they would write each other or visit each other when possible. Being youthful sometimes it is not difficult to be optimistic the day/night before Johnny was leaving toward his journey Jill would not leave for three months. There they both were going to the botanical gardens near their town loving {[passionately hugging kissing} ' on each other.

They went to a jazz set at some place it was really beautiful there near a lake that had a view outside you see the stars

This the wisdom not always right but for people all over the Global. James, Cynthia ofPotter House

Romance that has that expanded while of neither knew it would be creating a sustainability in both of us. Johnny got a another position . Lisa had to stay in her position.

The Continuous learning through came when Lisa met William during a summer1 session at the university most of their mutual friends were gone. We were both taking courses so we could graduate early. We meeting in various places having conversations about our ideas also dreams for when met hat we doing in our lives then also in the future. William had thousands of women that wanted to be with him because the way he looked not because his ideas with his contribution with his organization because of the conversations only William became the interested in Lisa unaware to her, the semester started ans Lisa was seeking a friend to assit her with statistic . she met a friend name Greggory he was very knowledgeable in this area. She met him mostly in the Library . on one occasion she went to met him at Greg apartment when she got there his room mate was William. William was so upset that I was there to see greg rather than him.

Little children, you are from God and have overcome them, for he who is in you is greater than he who is in the world Scripture : 1 John 4:4 ESV

Lisa had never met to hurt William unaware of his his was feeling. The friend ship was of value only fora season nota lifetime with him. Got to get an understanding of that more. William got that understanding eventually.

This hat season was short and the next semester started this was Lisa next to semester before becoming an graduate. Unforeseen to her she met a scholar in Dwight.

This relationship was more than Lisa coould can learn during their expecting . his contribution cause innovation, restoration, communication, with distribution.

T his ideal young male gave this to most men/womwen:

This the type of men/women you can learn from
She/man is unapologectically herself and radiates [positivity
Wherever she/her goes in life. He/she has been full of obstalces
He/she has overcome them all with the strength of a lioness .
He/she gives and gives without a hidden agenda and although
Can be buttally honest. He/she never Judges anyone . He/she is a
Natural born leade that has no patience for drama queens and
Takers he/she is both Holy fire and Hell water and the flavor
You taste depends on how she/he is being treated.

Lisa/Johnny building in Asian country their relationship during these systems . He/she flrting with disaster both of their Families expecting miracles coming /going While consistent motion. Johnny/Lisa

Were visiting the extravagant places Lisa/Johnny keeping their focuses neither considering the cultures

Both existing for above beyond their expectations. Keeping in mind the children adults men/boys women/girls they touch with collaboration while building > insert video with inspiration

NO MAN KNOWS BUT THE LORD-7sx

1 Authority {strength under control that must be harvested
A (commit t o God's Jesus rulers)
B. (it is strengthening udercontrol that shall be harvested
2. Sensitivity-Training area {close to to purpose you're purpose Father son Holy Sprit} se the
Formula:
O- not all about me M- umerit favor Grace I- In Jesus Christ N- near you/me JesusChrist O-oh hurts a little while U-undeniable near JESUS!
S-Significant other loves me /you
A.be close to the area whweere you suppose to be
B.You're not exactly purposeful sure yet
O- not all about you/me
3.Separation you're not sure where you are to go.
A. Youll can not see who exactly is to go.
B. Everybody can't can 't go where you are called to go.
C. Through The Lord God JESUS has a place destiny for you to go
4. Set Your own Stage
A. Trust God don't always wait for a handout (use this formula : O- oh not all about me/u
M-unmerit favor Grace I- in JESUS Christ N- near you/me is ESUS! CHRIST O- hurts alittle while
U- undeniable you/me S- significant to you other God/Lord loves me/u
5. Test Scrafice
A. Give up something you loves

The relationship (marriage was definitely near) Scripturise: Mark10:9 KJV with TESJ(Tony E). what god joins together let no one put a sunder.

> ➤ Note; formula

E - ever
Q - movethis quickly
U - Keep my head up seeking GOD
C - Around God's ominous

T - Total Praise keep praising
I - I Never Alone
O - Oh it hurts for a little
N - need my faith to raise

God is with us(the cultures of people of African decent includes Phillipans Asian Hispanic).

This is building living while in purpose . Scripture: 2 Corinthians 3:17 now the lord is the spirit and where the spirit of the lord is there is Freedom.

Now if the ministry that brought condemnation had glory, the ministry that brings righteousness overflows with even more glory . infact, what has been glorious has not been glorious by comparison because of the glory that surpasses it. 2 Corithians 3: 9-10 KJV TES(Tony Evans StudyBible)

The small battles in life prepares us for the big ones or even war . Give an example Of a time reasonly that I was a family member trying to controlling that I believe that

Romance that has that expanded while of neither m knew it would be creating a sustainability in both of us. Johnny got a another position . Lisa had to stay in her position.

The Continuous learning through came when Lisa met William during a summer1 session at the university most of their mutual friends were gone. We were both taking courses so we could graduate early. We meeting in various places having conversations about our ideas also dreams for whe met hat we doing in our lives then also in the future. William had thousands of women that wanted to be with him because the way he looked not because his ideas with his contribution with his organization because of the conversations only William became the interested in Lisa unaware to her, the semester started ans Lisa was seeking a friend to assit her with statistic . she met a friend name Greggory he was very knowledgeable in this area. She met him mostly in the Library . on one occasion she went to met him at Greg apartment when she got there his room mate was William. William was so upset that I was there to see greg rather than him.

Little children, you are from God and have overcome them, for he who is in you is greater than he who is in the world Scripture : 1 John 4:4 ESV

Lisa had never met to hurt William unaware of his his was feeling. The friend ship was of value only fora season nota lifetime with him. Got to get an understanding of that more. William got that understanding eventually.

That season was short and the next semester started this was Lisa next to last semester before becoming an graduate. Unforeseen to her she met a scholar in Dwight

Always Find Lesson ; The Perserverance Lesson: The story is love story

It began with a guy name Johnny He (Johnny showed her how seek the proper science with future. We sit in the various building on the University campus .

Furthermore the romance was starting neither of them knew what was happening focus on receiving their education. Sometimes johnny Lisa meet in the student Union Building (Aplace with resturants,executives, advisors, president /vice president offices,meeting areas, games areas ice palors) a learning center to expess our interest/love to each other. This was the start remember we were not us was aware of our affection

That
Nevertheless, we conversatons included interest such like community building,sciences, Arts, mathmechancal, etc. remembering that john,lisa from diffent family that dependent on them to achieve their learning so they could be superior in heir lives later.

p **Scripture: Jeremiah29:11 KJV TES(Tony Evans Study Bible)God knows the** you to lead you plans for you to prosper

The reason I am in this position is because during my maturity in your that grws into wisdom.0
This achievement allows you to have it all.

Spritual Growth (tossed like a salad)

My life receive the growth God (father son holy spirit gave could not see that my problems those principles learned most while serving in the position in ministry that during while praying studing to seeking God's face. Pouring myself out in ways that could be only describe as the anointing of the Holy spirit. My reasoning since I'm in this human body was struggle,fighting, battling waring with this Holy spirit that was/is on me. This part of myself as well with everybody, Recognizing, calling, praying, seeking allows the raising in of the spirit is the defining factor that everybody does not have in people

Scripture: John3:16 God so loved the world that he gave his only begotten son who believe in him will not perish but have everlasting life.

This is no boasting bragging or self proclaiming mostly this cause you to be breakin most often
Listen friends,relative,. Co-workersis only, presidents, CEOs will look at you crazy you'll find jobs, loose jobs
This anointing will shake you to your Core ! believe when I say you'll come out with the Victory!
In the Kingdom of God while living on this side of life,

Nevertheless you'll maybe have to battle/ war with fear, selfishness, jealousy, with me my spiritual war with unforgiveness. This is stronghold like I never seen in the 21St Century.
It cause death untold with virus that has gripped the world with a Pandemic.
This has broken people that previous thought they were in control .
God(Father son Holy spirit
Shows up in ways. Be encouraged that the impossible can turn around to an unexpected surprise in mine/your favorite. Scripture Hope through God's Grace Mercy: Litimentations 3:1 KJV TES I am
The man/woman that have seen affliction with God 's wrath.

The innovative process in more/ less consistence with inefficiency that requires many woman
With continuous communication. Abundance formula (means X outcomes + abundance that with innovation . Looking at the problems in the light means=funds,

This certain problem can be discriminatory(unfair prejudicial) elimination by active innovative
Cosmic Communication with collabration from people with various cultures, be the people with means(money or mental poor. Everyone on this one. Based on these current economics(a condition of a region in a season circumstances .
He

Title>Fact Check
Tor Example .
This significant relationship that with Johnny,Lisa blooming though out it involved us seeing as much as another with cpnversations. Nevertheless, that was growing in their purpose with being here at the university. T)hey (johnny Lisa)

Both involve in the socially economically, health, infurustructurally at their univerhey met in sity.
They would meet in his dorm with emotional,physically togetherness in ways that would be relaxing and fulfilling for them both(sexual emotionally, physically). They would meet in her dorm. Johnny,lisa
They meetin various events like social,econpminical, health, while the building went on at the university.

Everyone knew they were a couple so the challenge began ining the relationship
with them maintaining. Ohnny,lisa was in the fight of their lives began to under-s
standing the vital learning that they both had to go through. This is a marthorn not running
for it, enduring for the lifetime of the relationship while at the university.

At The Last we were with, Jill/Dwight are in Alaska and Johnny/Lisa are in Asia

Keep in mind that Jill/Johnny longing for the time they will return to each other.

Continue with their assignments while their (Jill, Johnny) achieving systems collaborations

The Continuous of both couples is ordered through that is greater than you/me the ominious formaula O- Oh it is not all about me

M - unmerited favor Grace
I - Jesus Christ in me
N - near Jesus around me
O - Oh! it hurts a little while
U - Undeniable Jesus is near
S - significant God loves you God loves me

This is the strategy to continue to keep Jill/Johnny in constant motion while their with significant people in life longing to be together in the future. They were restreaming themselves during the current position they were in with other people that was temporary

Little did they know while in their positions currently.

While there are in positions they(Jill/Dwight observing in flying over the area the other couple (Johnny/Lisa) in Asia durinsg the same. Building systems Domestic system Eclectric system Pediatrics systems

Nevertheless there Jill/Dwight in Alaska seeking collaboration observing touring enjoying

Listening though various modalities such as the people communities economic systems including biomedical aerospace electronic keeping continuity. Keep being aware that Johnny/ Lisa insia, Their positions a little while complicated though not less producing communities building in with systems for people living currently plus future. `

Always Fund the Lesson: PERSERVANCE JOURNEY
ROCHELLE KELLY
Westbow Press Affiliation

Persevance Paper

The couple Johnny,Jill was continuing their quest while youthful resilience in both still hopes to returning to each one soon. Their both in their position setting up systems.

Their both in unfamiliar surroundings while their friends family co-workers to achieve the completion the of system building. Keep in mind Jill/Dwight in Alaska

Johnny/Lisa in Asia while both[Jill/Johnny) still hoping to see be together.

> Nevertheless, continue Jill with Dwight getting systems such economical, financial biomedicail, electrical, aerospace These systems are the same systems that Johnny/Lisa were also established systems Asia,

Is the best of

This perserevance Journey with both johnny with Jill both reaching out with passion that can not be compared competed comprehened with the love grace hope demonstrated.

Their{Johnny Jill)loves hope grace orchestrates . being in an exploring adventure.

Jill, Dwight in are created systems in Alaska such as to be recognize while having them already in place.

While Johny,Lisa created systems in Asia Souel Korea while being not Compromising with Grace Love Hope with very Good outcomes with during connecting. They both{Johnny,Jill}were in constant motion in position longing for each other.

The distance seem to get insurmountable with there Faith rising that they both understanding that most would not understand. This is Faith rising again again again

This is excellence motion with Holy spirit of Jesus christ that is the Awesomeness. The fact of the matter is this is an motion that doesn't allow viscidity. During Johnny with Jill opening the many facilities. "HIS thoughts are HIGER AND GREATER THAN OURS'. Ewards. Cindy CRAZY FAITH

Their prospective are that they were in temporary overwhelming circumstances examples David

The High School Ups and downs wile achieving excellence was both jill/ johnny . This is the This is the best swith most diversity years the spirit of lord said count it all joy. What comes to mind about these ears several journey. Nevertheless. My high school was transitional for me with college during time I had a my best friend, I love this person prepare me what my future . Keep in mind were both involved in a religion at this time. This was both of our developing time to prepare for the milieu.

Although neither of us knew it then,. Jill/johnny were destiny. Reminding me of a time when he was called a mechanical man that what the call a unit in the ROTC in high school. These men in high school Juniors and seniors were the best precision when it cam to presenting the colors[flags} at the football basketball soccer hockey various sports events. His siter was a friend of m ine she did not attend the school where jill/johnny went during this time. He was so respectful to me at that time I was so young did not understand that most young his age was mostly just trying to have sex, he was so patient with mber I told he was sooooooo diffident I did not have anyone to compare him because I never gave anyone time to get close to me at that time. for We did have sex for awhile until I graduate. I was involved in many activities in orchestra, marching band, Speech drama club, student council, competing queen of school. Nevertheless also in prose, poetry and plays performance all over state, the thorn in my side was mother /father. I performed in one-act plays (Purlie Victorious) with this male friend of mind we practice so much with band practice, student counselinng very active. We preformed in the UIL competition. We performed won the UIL competion. Since it was only one trophy we argued about who would take it home so I told him if I could take it home for that day he could have it. This how I endure through insurmountable circumstances never not really looking for any positive feedback took the trophy to show my mother what I had been doing because if I had not it would have been very determental (fusing,spanking) she would 've acted like I did not tell her about the UIL competition, that is why how no matter excellent my presentation (spoken, writings, mathematics, acting)never looking for accolades when it does happen never especially from my family or love ones with me just go to the next venue in my living. Staying humble not getting puff up in pride staying with Lord Jesus God(father son Holy spirit I serve. This up bring that cause me to preserve

It was not meant to cause me determent in my personality it causes opposition with people but mostly with the family, friends, neighbors. This is raging that need to occur to create mechanism for strengthen in living in life. Sometimes it looks like you coming up against insurmountable odds but if you would step back use ominous formula currently in these unexpected occurrences

O- Oh! not all about me
M-unmerited favor ofGod's Grace
I-in me Jesus Christ
N-near me Jesus
O-Oh! it hurts a little while
U-undeniable God is with us
Significant- God loves me God loves you

Always Find the Lesson: Perseverance Journey

The johnny Lisa Journey after her travailing continuing with that excellent circumstances

Those issues are with testing still God(through Jesus Christ Nazareth) is incontrol while he living existence in various learning modalities listening,celebrations, visional

Mathematical. Johnny Lisa was the loves each other because of what was started in them by God through Jesus christ Nazareth

Nevertheless Johnny Lisa has gone their separate ways she made hope that they see each other again.

Nevertheless, john Lisa stay in their academic aknolegementthat made their lives worth living

This is the admiration that they both had fpr citcumstances great than themselves, yet this while couple never gave up longing with each other and without each other. The epic was example,

When she had to to come up in conference with him. (The victory while in the valley during the valley t this is temporary the scripture used Acts 6-7 Ryrie KJV The word of God increased and the number of disciples multiplied in Jersalem greatly and a great company of the priests were obedient to the faith.

Love that Johnny Lisa expand during the test trying to see if they could live with while growing in their lives.

Football Spirit Runs deep in the Bear Cave!!

The Bears Take Over the Frisco STAR Stadium!!

Happy Holiday
gankoff and
security aid

CONGRATS

DERRION

South Oak Cliff
claiming their
undefeated status
once again.

8

9

Daily Inspiration

BY ROCHELLE KELLY

November 30. 2021
Today's release Lord God through Jesus Christ Let the hope you/me
Continue the Joy Peace with God through Jesus Christ
Be Glorify Facing uncertainty

December 02, 2021
Today's release Lord God through jesus christ God is with you/me .
when the Holy Spirit covers us
Let us build confidence in knowing that God is with you/me inspired
by Luke 1;26-38

January 01, 2022
Today's release Lord God through Jesus Christ God has reconciliation
with you'll. The Lord sent only begotten son Messiah to reconcile me/
you inspired encourage in Grace with Love Be Glorify

January 02, 2022
Today's release Lord father God through Jesus Chris the steadfast
commitments that only God through Jesus christ helps you/me endure
keeping the full armor on through the word of God the ones that boast
should not in other words do not boast about what God is doing in your
life. Continue Blessings

January 03,2022
Todays release Lord God through Jessus christ Let's stay focus on our purpose while disappointments may have to go into seclusion for a moment to refocus God the Holy spirit allows be Glorify

January 04, 2022
Today's release Lord God through Jessus Christ reminded hat our testimony is what Jesus want you/me
To talk to people can see BEwhat God has done in our lives Example Jesus gives use the man with legions of demons on him and how they {Demons} were removed the Grace of God still exist today in the present. Be Glorified

January 05, 2022
Love, Joy. Peace, patience, kindness, goodness, and self Control, to these commit your day

January 06,2022
Todays release Lord God through Jesus Christ the plan with fruits of the spirit Love Joy Peace Patience Goodness Faithfulness self-control equal Grace. Get an understanding with your living suggestion yield your plans to God for a little while Because God taking care of those circumstances Be Glorify

January 07, 2022
Today's release Lord God through Jesus Christ although most of you know this we(you/me)
Are saved by Grace (unmerited favor) not by works (not by your might nothing you can do only God gives Grace . God is Father son Holy spirit Be Glorify

January 08, 2022
Today's release Lord God through Jesus Christ Let's believe in seeking Jesus not get caught in so many ministries or corporate living that we don't seek God Be Glorify ot you, me

January 09, 2022
Today's release Lord God through Jesus christ focus on Jesus not your circumstances that is temporary . God is moving onyour behalf you can not see it Let's your continuous Faith raise God is moving on your Behalf you can not see it God through Jesus christ got you Be Glorify

January 10, 2022
Joy you get from within the Holy Spirit of God dwelling in you. That way if you do not have more .Joy as you near to God Holy spirit of Jesus draws closer to you. You need to check your spiritual life

January 11,2022
Today's release Lord God through Jesus Christ Let God reign over every circumstance inn your Life.
Then you believe anything is possible with God {Father son Holy Spirit Jesus reign in yours mine lives Be Glorify

January 12, 2022
Today's release Lord God through Jesus christ put on your full armor of God the during times word
During times of troubles. Not fighting people but principality of darkness in the heavenly realms .inspired by Ephesians 6;10-16
Ing

January 13, 2022
Today's release Lord God through Jesus Christ wait on the Lord going through the process that better than anything that you can think of even Jesus had to wait thirty years before he could start his ministry Daniel had to wait in the Lion's den. Sarah and Abraham had to wait can be our greatest weakness when seeking God wait Trust God Be Glorify

January 14, 2022
Today's release Lord God through Jesus Christ Trust in God because is an everlasting rock. The Lord will keep you in pease inspired by Isiah 26;1-4

January 15, 2022
Today's release Lord God through Jesus christ prayers hold on to Gay's release Lord God through Jesus christ is there anything too hard for the Lord ? No Example Abraham, Sarah after they were old God showed up and answered their prayers The Awesome Holy Spirit oF God still answering your prayers Hold on to God's unchanging ways. Lord Gimes Let

January 16, 2022
patience
Today's release Lord God gives rest during the the valley times in our lives
Shepard lead you through the shadow of death Let the Shepard restore your soul
Inspired by Psalms 23 Be Glorify

January 17, 2022
Today's release Lord God through Jesus Christ contlinue to believe that the Holy spirit has all power to let us forgive those have wrong us God has the power to move fears give patience work within us Be Glorify

January 20, 2022
Today's release Lord God through Jesus christ do not be anxious for anything got to payer with supplication make our request known also give it to God think on the lovely know that God got your request

January 21.2022
Today's release Lord God through Jesus christ put on the full amor of GodFather son Holy Spirit}{so you may with stand this evil. We do not fight with flesh but principalities in theheavenly realms, Keep prayering in spirit to Jesus Continue to believe God is in control. Inspired by Ephesian6: 10-18

January 22,2022
Today's release Lord God through Jesus Christ reminder that we have the Holy Spirit to fight our battles that we can not see most of the time

we have to go in prayers for God to intercede Continue to believe God is in Control.

January 23, 2022
Today's release Lord God through Jessus chris to simple leave a place in our hearts for Jesus to dwell also to linger in you/me Be Gorify

January 24,2022
Today's release Lord God through Jesus Christ Let Faith rise in your life God will guide you through your known and unknown circumstances of your like give it to God let you Faith rise Example when Jesus told the widow also son to full vessel with oil and sale it and pay their debts. inspired by 2 king 4:1-7

January 25, 2022
Release Lord God through Jesus christ the Lord Jesus Christ Let my Faith Continue to rise my Hope in Jesus for the circumstances I can not see but hopeful that the Holy spirit of God is working on my behalf

January 26. 2022
Today's release lord God through Jesus christ the Lord gives you rest during the valley times in our lives l through the shadows of death. Let the shepard restore your soul Inspired by Psalms 23 Be Glorify

January 27,2022
Today's release Lord God through Jesus Christ Do not believe the lies of Satan God shows up when
We are physically, financially, emotionally and relationally when we are weak God {Father son Holy spirit} will manfest strength in you inspired by 2 Corinthians 12:6-12

January 28, 2022
Today's release Lord God through Jesus Christ let's daily let your Faith rise so you will do what God is asking you to do Example like Enoch walked daily with God and did not experience going

January 29, 2022
Today's release Lord God through Jesus Christ consider all Joy while going through trials because God is Faithful to deliver you from it all. Perservance must finish it work so you can mature. Trust God let your Faith rise inspired James 1:2-8 od
Concerns or wprries to God through Jesus CHRIST this day letting my faith

January 30, 2022
The Lord gives his people perpetual joy when the walk in obedience to him by D.L. Moody

January 31, 2022
Today's Release Lord God through Jesus Christ Giving all my concerns or worries to God through Jesus Christ this day letting my Faith rise Trust in God{Father son Holy spirit} have all worries at God ;s feet so my seed through the word of God grows in you/me.
od

February 01,2022
Today's release Lord God through Jesus christ do not worry or be anxious for nothing does worrying change anything? God can take care of all circumstances like God takes care of the birds do you see them worried about anything you are more value than any sparrows Give it to God today, inspired by Mathew 6: 25-33

February 02,2022
Today;s release Lord God through Jesus Christ here again put on the yolk of God{Father son Holy spirit} confess your sins because God's yolk is easy burdens are light the lord can will handle it all you/me more valuable to God inspired by Mathew 11:28-30

February 03, 2022
Today's release Lord God through Jesus Christ go deep with ourselves ask the Holy Spirit of Jesus Christ

February 04. 2022
That comfort you to remove that deep sins of the pass that self, family so you can continue to be in humility both externally also internally inspired by James3:9-12

February 05,2022
Today's release Lord God through Jesus Christ The Holy spirit is working throughout our lives with fellow believers like those stories in scriptures the Lord is our Ultimate rescuer . The Holy Spirit of Jesus Christ can be Trusted to save us from our sins throughout our circumstances .

February 06, 2022
Today's release Lord God through Jesus Chris God wants you to focus on your resources and what you do have rather than what you do not have A lesson in faith though Jesus Christ a again trust the lord let your faith rise. Inspired by number1:1-4

February 07, 2022
Today's release Lord God through Jesus Christ Continue to stay in God;s plan for your lives .Example look at El[jah when God's plan mantifested it was not what he though what he though he ran God showed up and saved Elijah God's plan was better Trust God go Inspired by 1King 19:1-5

February 08, 2022
Today's release Lord God through Jesus Christ God still has a plan for those that are call to God's purpose reminder God the lord loves you. Inspired Romans 8: 28-30

February 09,2022
Today's release Lord God through Jesus christ God's already working on your behave all your circumstances in life. Although I can see it right now. Example Job life story Continue to let your Faith rise In Jesus Christ God is in control Be Glorify

February 10,2022
Today's release lord God through Jesus Christ God is working on your behave when you give up on knowing all the details continue your Faith continue your faith rise have a Holy confidence that this will be a Good outcome .inspired by Genesis 37; 25-35

February 11, 2022 OD IS
Today's release Lord God through Jesus Christ Transgressions shame can be a constant no matter how our devotion to the Lord God though Jesus God is ominous stay still let your faith rise with Grace

February 12,2022
Today's release Lord God through Jesus Christ It is not that you doubt God's presences the plan of God
When you can not understand what God is doing God see what we can not God is our friend and Savior Trust God do not lean on your own understanding.

February 13,2022
Today's release Lord God through Jesus Chris Continue to stay in humbleness Trust God while seeking
God is sovereign you will not be brought Fear Shame Anger in Jesus Christ name.

February 14, 2022
Today's release Lord God through Jesus Christ it is nor you doubt God's presence the plan of God when you can not understand what the Lord is doing. God can see what you can not see. Lord is our savior our friend continue to trust the Lord do not lean on your own understanding.

February 15, 2022
Today's release Lord God through Jesus Christ you do not have to fit in you belong to Jesus christ a child of the most high God while it seems like you are struggling alone reminder that you already have faith and Future Trust in God

February 16. 2022

Today's release Lord God Through Jesus Christ do not let the circumstances of life press on you give it all to God Blessings continue Trust God

February 17, 2022

"No Healthy Christian ever chooses suffering he chooses God's will as Jesus did whether it means suffering or not" Oswald Chambers

Bibliography

Becoming Obama, Michelle
A Promise Land Obama< inkBarack
God Came Near Lucado Maximillo
Victory is Yours Jakes, T. D.
www.richdad,com
Poetry& Works Written& Illustration
kby Kelly Christopher E.
Shooting the Sacred Cows of Money
DOCUMENTARY ON FINICIAL EDUCATION THE
by Kiyosaki Robert
JOY IN MY LIFE Spurgeon, Charles
The Clever Factory Nashville
THE ART SCIENCE OF RESPECT Prince, James
THE SYSTEM BUIDER NGUYEN, XUANit
All verse adapted from the
King James Version of Holy Bible Choose Hope
"CRAZY FAITH" CINDEY J. EDWARDS
The GRAVE ROBBER BATTERSON MARK
Choose Hope King James Version of Holy Bible
E HOW TO STAY CHRISTIAN IN COLLEGE BUDZEWSKI J.

About the Author

Rochelle W. Kelly is the fourth child of siblings. She is also a mother, sister, daughter with a Graduate of Science degree in Speech and Language Pathology from Texas A&M University Commerce TX. Rochelle Kelly is someone from whom you can learn activity of life.

I have diversified into a company D&C Communicaide LLC building self esteem in individuals to build and confidence through communication applications.

Printed in the United States
by Baker & Taylor Publisher Services